NATIONAL GEOGRAPHIC

Ladders

Welcome to Kenya

AROUND THE WORLD

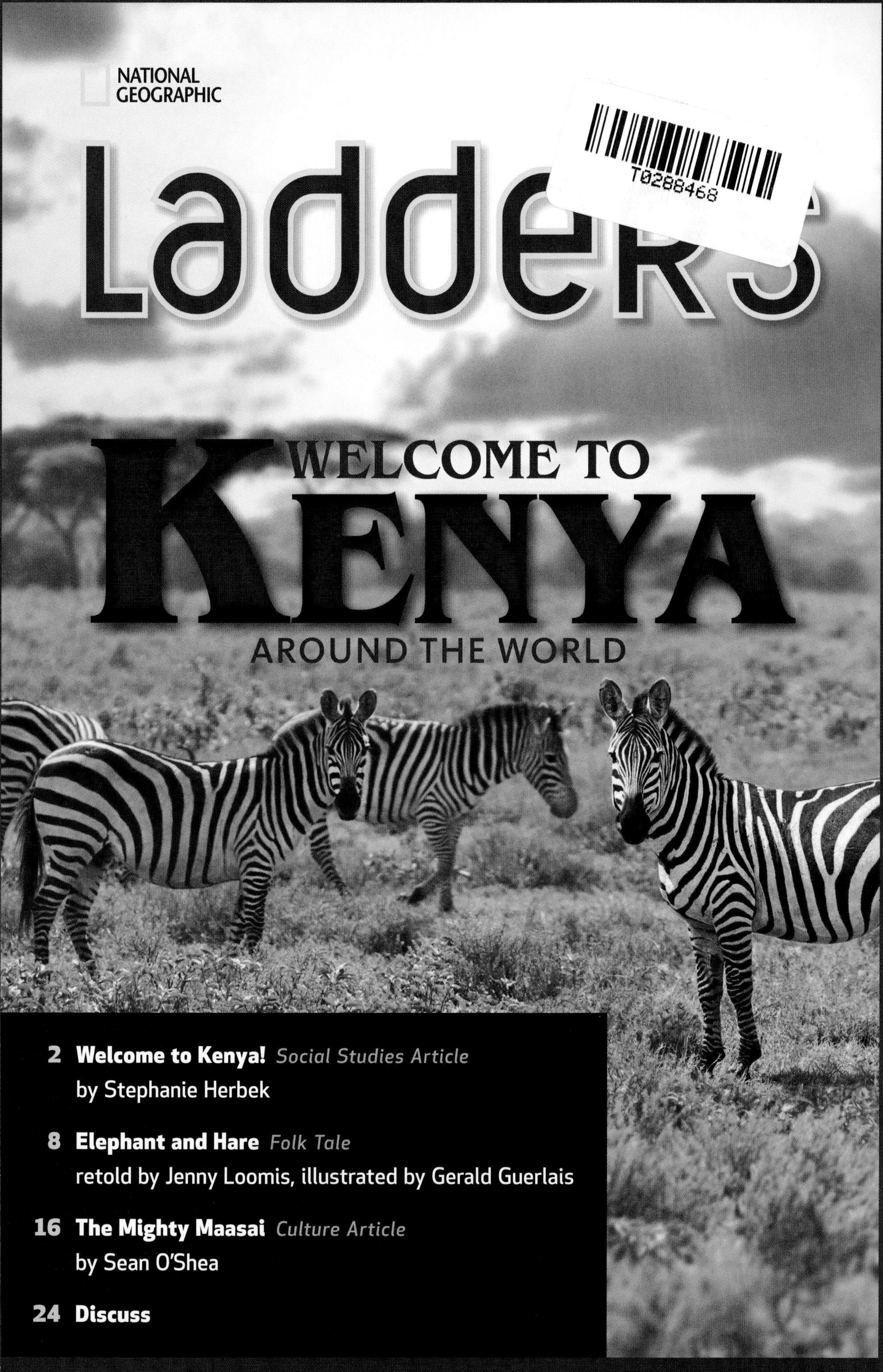

Welcome to KENYA!

by Stephanie Herbek

Kenya is a country in Africa. Most days there are hot, dry, and sunny. Cheetahs, elephants, giraffes, and many other animals live on **savannas**, or lands covered with grasses and other plants. They find shade under leafy trees that hide them from the bright sun.

These cheetahs live in the grassy savannas of Kenya. Cheetahs can run 70–75 miles an hour. Female cheetahs often have three babies at a time.

Animals aren't the only living things in Kenya. More than 40 million people live there, too. Most of them live in **villages**. A village is a community that is smaller than a city and is usually located in the country. Many people who live in villages work on farms. They spend many hours planting crops in their fields.

Other Kenyans live in the city. They take a bus or drive cars on busy streets to get to their jobs. They work in offices, factories, and schools. Let's find out more about the people and communities of Kenya.

Straw Huts and Skyscrapers

The Kenyans in some villages live with their **tribes**. A tribe is a group of people with the same language, way of life, and beliefs. Most villagers live in comfortable huts made of sticks and mud. A fire pit in the middle of each hut is used to cook food and heat water for washing. Villagers get water from deep underground wells.

Villagers keep very busy working on their farms. They grow much of the food they eat, such as cassava. Cassava is a vegetable that is a little like a potato. Villagers also care for their cows and goats. These animals give villagers milk to sell in markets and to drink.

Kenyan huts are designed well. Their straw roofs shelter people from the hot sun. Huts also keep villagers dry when it rains.

People sell their crops and farm animals at markets. This colorful market is in the center of a Kenyan village.

Some Kenyans live in cities such as Nairobi (nih-ROH-bee), the capital of Kenya. Nairobi is the largest city in the country. More than three million people live there. This city is a lot like big cities in other parts of the world. It has libraries, skyscrapers, and restaurants. Most people in Nairobi live in apartment buildings or houses made of flat sheets of metal. Some drive minivans, and others ride motorcycles or bikes.

Some parts of Nairobi, Kenya, are green and full of trees. Other parts of the city are full of tall buildings and cars.

Time for School, Time for Fun

Most children who live in Kenyan villages walk to school every morning. The day starts with a song, and then students learn Swahili (swuh-HEE-lee). This is the language that people speak in Kenya and in many other African countries. The students study outside at tables under trees. Sometimes they can hear the sound of birds chirping during their lessons. It must be fun to share a classroom with animals!

Not all children go to school in their village. Some of them go to schools far away from home. Other children help with farmwork instead of going to school.

Schools in the cities of Kenya are like many in the United States. Some students wear uniforms to school. Others wear regular clothes. The children work at tables in large classrooms. At some city schools, students use computers. Just like you, students may walk or take a bus to and from school.

The weather in Kenya is sunny and warm. It is perfect for playing outside. What sports do Kenyan children play? They love to play soccer, basketball, and volleyball.

Say it in Swahili

tafadhali (TAH-fah-DAH-lee) means "please"
asante (ah-SAHN-tay) means "thank you"
Habari? (hah-BAR-ee) means "How are you?"
kwaheri (kwah-HAIR-ee) means "good-bye"

Some classes in Kenya are held outdoors. Imagine seeing an elephant walk by while you are at school!

Check In How is school in Kenya different from what school is like where you live? How is it similar?

Elephant and Hare

a Traditional Kenyan Folk Tale

retold by Jenny Loomis *illustrated by Gerald Guerlais*

*A folk tale is a story that teaches **values**, or beliefs about what is important and how people should behave. This folk tale is from Kenya. The elephant in this story stands for strength. A **hare** is an animal like a rabbit, but bigger. The hare in this story stands for **cleverness**, or intelligence. Some folk tales explain why animals look the way they do. This folk tale explains why hares have short tails.*

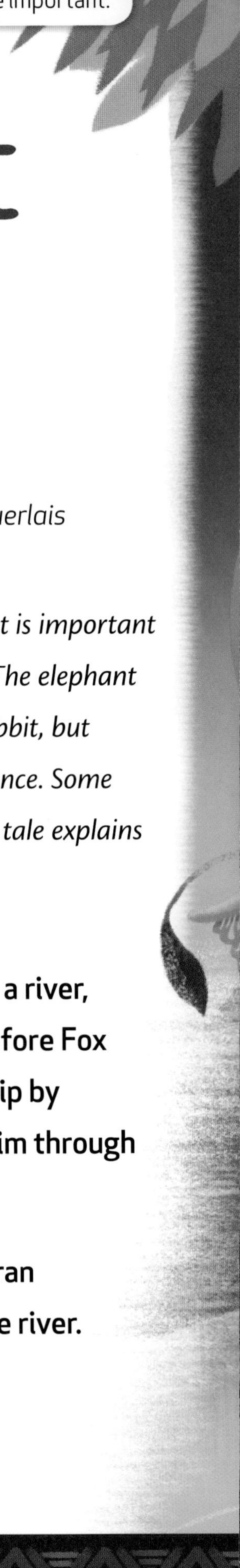

As day was turning to night, Hare stood at the edge of a river, looking down at the water. She needed to get home before Fox came out for his nightly hunt. She could shorten her trip by crossing the river. But she wasn't strong enough to swim through the deep water.

Just then, Elephant came running across the field. He ran up to Hare and laughed at her. "I see you can't cross the river. That's too bad, because swimming is so easy for me!"

"Elephant, please wait," said Hare. "Could I ride on your back as you swim across the river? I'm afraid Fox will find me before I can get home to give my children this big pot of honey." Hare opened her basket and showed Elephant a pot of honey.

Elephant smiled when he saw the honey. It was his favorite sweet treat. He could eat honey all day, every day.

"I will carry you across the river if you give me your honey pot," Elephant said.

"But this honey is a gift for my children," said Hare sadly.

"Fine. Then I am leaving. Say 'hello' to Fox for me," said Elephant meanly.

Hare knew she had to get home before dark, so she quickly came up with a clever plan. "Okay, you can have the honey," said Hare.

"That's a very smart choice, Hare. Hop on so we can get going!" Elephant ordered.

Elephant carried Hare across the river. When they reached the other side, he lifted his trunk up over his head to get the honey pot. Instead, Hare put an empty cup into Elephant's trunk. Then she jumped off his back and ran toward her home. Elephant was busy admiring his powerful trunk so he didn't notice that Hare had fooled him.

When he saw he had been tricked, Elephant was angry. He threw the empty cup on the ground and chased after Hare. His strong legs took him closer and closer. Hare jumped into a hole, but Elephant reached out and grabbed her long tail. Hare's long, fluffy tail snapped off. She was left with nothing but a puff.

Surprised, Elephant threw the tail down. He stuck his trunk into the hole to try to reach Hare, but it became caught in a tree root. Hare escaped while Elephant was busy trying to free his trunk. She ran to a large group of hares standing nearby.

Hare knew that she couldn't hide from Elephant for very long. She needed to blend in with the other hares, but they all had long tails. Then Hare thought of a clever way to blend in. She hid her basket in some bushes and joined the group of hares. She yelled, "Quickly! Take off your long tails! Elephant is coming and he's very angry. He's looking for hares with long tails!"

The scared hares had just pulled off their long tails when Elephant arrived. He was very angry. He didn't like being tricked by a little hare. He wanted that honey now more than ever. He screamed, "I'm looking for the hare with the short tail! Hares with long tails must step to one side."

The group of hares slowly turned around and showed Elephant their short tails.

"Oh! That hare has tricked me again!" grumbled Elephant. Fed up with clever hares, Elephant stomped away.

Hare picked up her basket and ran home as fast as she could. When she got there, she fed her hungry children the honey. Then she showed them her new, short tail. The children liked her tail so much that they decided to shorten their own tails.

Hare also told her children about the elephant. "Children, you may not be as big and strong as other animals, but you are very smart. When you get into trouble, try to think of a solution. Just being big or strong won't solve all your problems."

The children were thankful they had such a smart mother. They each gave her a big hug. Then they ate the rest of the yummy honey.

Check In How does Hare trick Elephant?

GENRE Culture Article

Read to find out about the Maasai people of Kenya.

If you visit Kenya's savanna, you may see a man dressed in bright red clothing walking through the grass. He's most likely a Maasai (muh-SY) man, walking with a herd of cattle, or cows. The Maasai people live in Kenya. They are **nomads**, which means they move from place to place. They move to find places with fresh grass for their cattle to eat.

Maasai men have to walk many miles each day. They must move their cattle to grassy areas.

The Mighty M

The Maasai treat their cattle very well. Maasai men are usually in charge of the herds. They often give their cows names. Sometimes they sing to them! The Maasai think of their cows as family members. The cattle are given this special treatment because they give the Maasai what they need to live good, comfortable lives. Cows provide the Maasai with milk, meat, and leather. They are very useful animals.

asai

by Sean O'Shea

Milk, Meat, and Medicine

The Maasai don't eat their cows' meat very often. They only eat the meat during special celebrations. The cows' milk is very important to the Maasai because it makes up most of their diet. Milk is a common meal for the Maasai. They also use milk to make other foods.

In the morning, some Maasai drink milk or spiced milky tea called *chai* (CHY). Many Maasai eat a porridge made from corn flour, milk, water, and sugar. They call this porridge *ugi*. The Maasai also eat yogurt made from their cows' milk.

Sometimes the Maasai nibble on tree bark between meals. That might seem strange to you. But if you've eaten anything with cinnamon in it, you've eaten tree bark, too. The Maasai use tree bark to flavor soup, the way you might use cinnamon to add flavor to oatmeal. They also use tree bark as medicine for an upset stomach.

< Owning cattle is a lot of work. Maasai men spend their days herding the animals. Maasai women milk the cattle twice a day.

How to Make Kenyan Chai Tea

Chai tea is a very popular drink in Kenya. It is tea mixed with milk, sugar, and spices. Many children drink chai in the morning before going to school.

1. Pour 2 cups of water and 2 cups of milk into a saucepan.
2. Add 1½ teaspoons of black tea leaves (or more, if you like strong tea) to the water and milk in the saucepan.
3. Add some spices such as cinnamon, cardamom, and ginger to the saucepan.
4. With an adult's help, bring the mixture to a boil.
5. Turn the heat down and mix the tea with a spoon until it tastes strong enough.
6. Add a little sugar to sweeten the tea, and stir.
7. Remove the tea leaves from the saucepan.
8. Pour the spiced tea into a mug and enjoy!

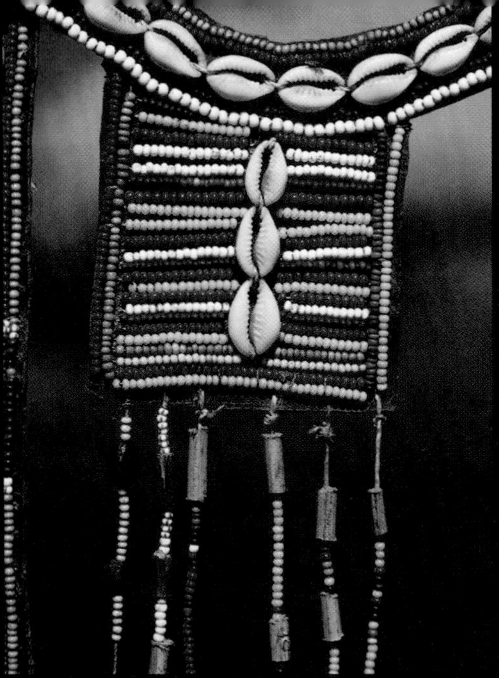

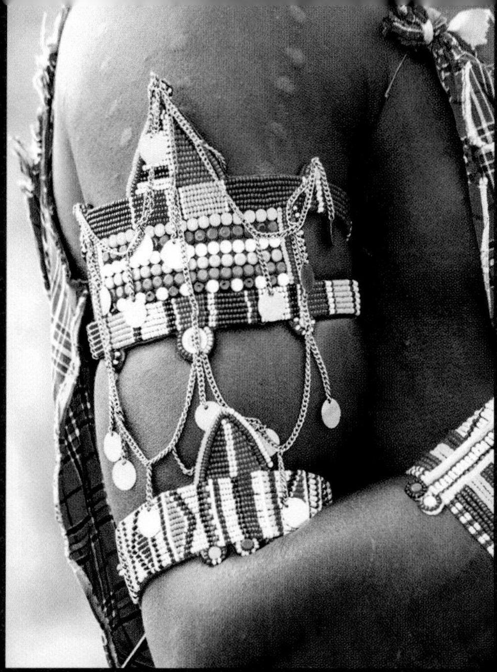

The Power of Red

The Maasai wear clothing that keeps them cool and comfortable in Kenya's warm weather. Their clothing and shoes are often made from animal skins. They also wear cotton because it keeps them cooler. The Maasai's villages are far away from markets, so they even make some clothes out of things they find near their homes. For example, some Maasai make sandals out of old car tires. The Maasai like to wear brightly colored clothing. Red is an important color to them because it **symbolizes**, or stands for, power.

The Maasai make beautiful jewelry in many different colors. They use glass and clay beads as **ornaments**, or things that add beauty. They also string together metal, seeds, ivory, bone, horns, shells, leather, and feathers. The Maasai wear this jewelry in the form of earrings, necklaces, and bracelets. Sometimes young men and women wear special jewelry to attract each other.

Jumping for Joy

Jumping is part of a Maasai dance called *adumu*. In this dance, warriors take turns jumping. A Maasai **warrior** is a young man who learns how to hunt and how to protect his family. Each warrior sings as he jumps higher and higher. The man who jumps the highest wins the contest. The Maasai believe that the highest jumper is the strongest warrior.

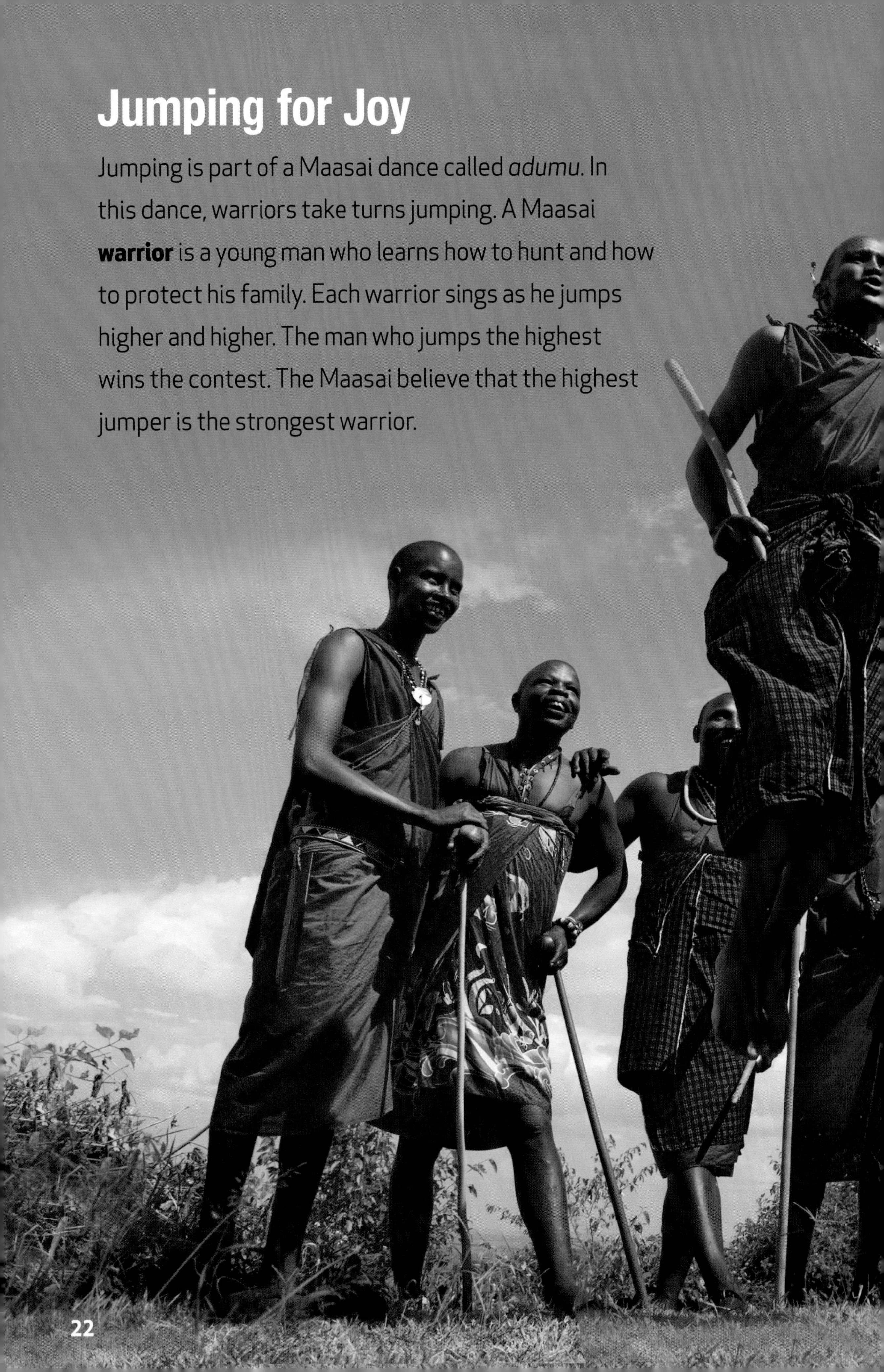

Maasai males become warriors when they are in their teens. After about ten years of being warriors, they are ready to become adults. They dance to celebrate the end of their warrior years and the beginning of adulthood. Once they are adults, the men can get married, have a family, and raise cows.

Two Maasai warriors show their strength by jumping high into the air.

Check In Why are cattle important to the Maasai?

Discuss

1. Tell about some of the ways you think the three selections in this book are linked.

2. How is living in a village in Kenya different from living in a city?

3. What are some important things you have learned about the Maasai way of life?

4. In the folk tale, Hare is clever and Elephant is strong. Do you think cleverness or strength is more important? Why?

5. What do you still wonder about Kenya and the people who live there?